I0479784

SKYROCKET YOUR
BUSINESS REACH:

A Step-by-Step Guide to Drive
Conversions and Boost Sales.

Sam Austin

TABLE OF CONTENTS

Chapter 1
Chapter 2
Chapter 3
Chapter 4
Chapter 5
Chapter 6
Chapter 7
Chapter 8
Chapter 9
Chapter 10
Chapter 11
Chapter 12
Chapter 13
Chapter 14
Conclusion

PART A

THE SCOPE OF

SOCIAL MEDIA

MARKETING

Chapter 1

Definition of Social Media Marketing

Social media marketing is the practice of using websites and social media networks to advertise a good or service. Social media marketing is growing in popularity among practitioners and researchers, even though the terms e-marketing and digital marketing continue to be dominant in academia. The majority of social media platforms come with built-in data analytics tools that let businesses monitor the development, effectiveness, and engagement of marketing campaigns.

Through social media marketing, businesses communicate with a variety of stakeholders, including current and potential employees, journalists, bloggers, and the general public. In terms of strategy, social media marketing entails managing a marketing campaign, determining the scope (for example, whether to use social media actively or passively), and establishing the social media "culture" and "tone" that a company wants to adopt.

Businesses can use social media marketing to let customers and internet users post user-generated content, also referred to as "earned media" (e.g., online comments, product reviews, etc.), as opposed to using a copy that has been created by marketers for advertising.

Participation in the social network

Customers and stakeholders who use the social website actively participate rather than view it as passive audience members. These include organizations that advocate for consumers and those that criticize businesses (such as lobbying or advocacy groups). All customers/citizens can express and share their opinions about a company's products, services, business practices, or government actions when social media is used in a business or political context.

Every customer who participates As other customers read their positive or negative comments or reviews, a non-customer or citizen who is participating online via social media becomes a part of the marketing department (or a challenge to the marketing effort). Successful social media marketing depends on engaging clients, potential clients, or citizens online. With the advent of social media marketing, it has become increasingly important to gain customer interest in products and services. This can eventually be translated into buying behavior or voting and donating behavior in a political context. To increase customer participation and brand reputation, new concepts of engagement and loyalty in online marketing have emerged.

Social media use is divided into two categories for a social media strategy. The first is proactive, frequent publication of fresh online content. Digital images, videos, texts, and conversations all demonstrate this. The dissemination of information and content from other sources via web links is another example of it.

The second type of conversation is reactive, where users of social media reply to messages or comments made on your social media profiles. Traditional media, like TV news programs, are restricted to one-way interactions with consumers, or "push and tell," where only specific information is provided to the consumer and there are few or no mechanisms in place to solicit feedback. It is possible for readers of traditional media, like printed newspapers, to submit a letter to the editor. The editorial board must review the letter and determine whether it should be published, which is a relatively slow process. On the other hand, social media is participatory and open; participants can instantly share their views on brands, products, and services. Traditional media gave control of the message to the marketer, whereas social media shifts the balance to the consumer or citizen.

Chapter 2

The Purpose of Social Media Marketing

Utilizing social media as a communications tool to make businesses visible to those who are unfamiliar with their products and accessible to those who are interested in them is one of the main goals of using social media in marketing. These businesses target their customers through social media, generate buzz about themselves, and learn from them. It is the only type of marketing that can interact with customers at every phase of their decision-making process.

Other advantages of social media marketing exist as well. Seven of the top 10 elements that influence a successful Google organic search depend on social media. As a result, companies that are less active on social media or do not use it at all tend to show up less frequently on Google searches. The visual media sharing mobile platforms, however, have a higher interaction rate in comparison, have seen the fastest growth, and have altered how consumers engage with brand content, even though platforms like Twitter, Facebook, and Google+ have more monthly users.

Instagram has an interaction rate of 1.46% with an average of 130 million users monthly, as opposed to Twitter, which has a 0.03% interaction rate with an average of 210 million monthly users. Unlike traditional media, which is often cost-prohibitive for many companies, a social media strategy does not require astronomical budgeting.

To achieve this, businesses use platforms like Facebook, Twitter, YouTube, TikTok, and Instagram to reach audiences much wider than they could have done with just traditional print, TV, and radio advertisements, and at a fraction of the cost (although some websites charge businesses for premium services). As a result, businesses now approach customer interactions differently because a sizable portion of consumer interactions now take place on online platforms with much higher visibility.

Through social media platforms, customers can now post reviews of goods and services, rate customer service, ask questions, and voice concerns to businesses. According to Measuring Success, more than 80% of consumers do their product and service research online. Businesses use social media marketing in this way to establish trusting relationships with customers. Companies may also employ individuals to handle these social media interactions specifically; these individuals typically report under the title of "online community managers." Consumer confidence can rise if these interactions are handled satisfactorily. Three steps are taken to address consumer concerns to accomplish this goal and improve the public's perception of a company: determining the scope of the social chatter, enlisting the assistance of influencers, and developing a proportionate response.

Chapter 3

Platforms and Metrics

1. Facebook

Facebook enables businesses to post videos, pictures, longer descriptions, and testimonials. Additionally, customers can leave comments on the product pages for other users to see. As of May 2015, 93% of businesses' marketing departments used Facebook to promote their brands. According to a 2011 study, Facebook advertising was responsible for 84% of "engagement," or links to clicks and likes. Facebook started limiting the content that could be posted on brand and business pages in 2014. Facebook made changes to its algorithms in February 2014 that reduced the audience for non-paying business pages (with at least 500,000 "likes") from 16% in 2012 to 2%.

2. LinkedIn

LinkedIn is a website for networking between professionals in the business world. Companies can use it to build professional profiles for both themselves and their company. Members can advertise their various social networking activities on their LinkedIn profile page by using widgets, such as their Twitter stream or blog posts about their product pages. Members of LinkedIn have the chance to find business partners and sales leads. Members can create "Company Pages," which are like Facebook pages and give business owners a place to advertise their goods and services and engage with customers.

3. Instagram

Instagram had more than 200 million users as of May 2014. Instagram had a user engagement rate that was 15 times greater than Facebook's and 25 times greater than Twitter. The most recent studies suggest that 93% of prestige brands have an active presence on Instagram and include it in their marketing mix, according to Scott Galloway, the founder of L2 and a professor of marketing at New York University's Stern School of Business.

Instagram's mission when it comes to brands and businesses is to support businesses in reaching their target audiences through compelling imagery in a vibrant, visual environment. Additionally, Instagram offers a channel for open communication between users and businesses, making it a perfect channel for businesses to engage with both current and potential clients.

Instagram has established itself as a powerful platform for marketers to connect with their clients and prospects by sharing images and inspirational messages. According to a Simply Measured study, 71% of the world's biggest brands are currently using Instagram as a marketing channel. Instagram can be used by businesses as a tool to connect and communicate with both current and potential clients.

The brand can be portrayed more personally by the company, which improves and more accurately represents the company. Instagram photos have the "on-the-go" concept, which gives the impression that the event is taking place right now. This adds another level to the accurate and personal representation of the business.

Instagram gives businesses the chance to accurately represent their brand from the viewpoint of their customers, for instance by using user-generated content and encouraging hashtag usage. In addition to the filters and hashtags features, Instagram's 15-second videos and the recently added feature that allows users to send private messages to one another have created new opportunities for brands to connect with customers in new ways, further promoting efficient marketing on Instagram.

Metrics

1. Online reports

This entails monitoring the number of visits, leads, and customers that come from each specific social channel to a website. Google

Analytics is a free tool that displays the behavior of website visitors from social networks as well as additional data, including demographics and the type of device used. Marketers can choose the most effective social networks and social media marketing campaigns with the help of offers like these from companies.

2. Data on return on investment

Any marketing effort's ultimate objective is to produce sales. Even though social media is a helpful marketing tool, it can be challenging to measure how much it boosts revenue. ROI can be calculated by comparing a contact database or CRM's marketing analytic value and directly linking marketing initiatives to sales activity.

3. Rates of customer response

Many consumers are using social media to express their admiration for or annoyance with particular brands, products, or services. As a result, marketers can assess the effectiveness of their social media marketing strategies by tracking the frequency with which consumers talk about their brand. According to recent studies, 72% of those polled said they expected a Twitter reply to their complaints within an hour.

PART B

FACEBOOK

ADVERTISEMENTS

Chapter 4

Introduction

Facebook Advertisements is the social network's advertising platform that aims to advertise goods and services through publications or text, image, or video advertisements. Because of the size of its audience (roughly 2,200 million) and the numerous segmentation options, it is a marketing channel that is frequently used by businesses.

Facebook has created targeting technology that enables advertisements to target a particular group of people. This is a feature of the Facebook Ads product, which is accessible to both users and companies. An advertiser is given a list of qualities that will define his target market when posting an advertisement through the Facebook Ad Manager. This is what Facebook calls audience targeting. Geographic location and interests like music are just a few of these characteristics.

According to Facebook, advertisers can even tailor their target audience based on people's behavior, including their buying habits, device usage, and other habits. Due to this, Facebook users see ads on their profile pages that are pertinent to their tastes and passions. This makes it possible for the advertisements to be less intrusive and more effective at reaching the right audience with the right content. The advertising algorithm can also track performance, allowing advertisers or Facebook marketers to change their target audience as well as the type, price point, and duration of the ads based on how well they are performing.

Based on Facebook advertising statistics, the most important information for managing a successful and profitable Facebook advertising campaign is provided below:

a. Facebook ads are incredibly effective.
b. Simple setup and quick results
c. 1.73 billion users are active each day
d. Mobile accounts for 94% of Facebook's ad revenue.
e. The average conversion rate for Facebook ads across all industries is 9.21%.
f. The typical CPC and CPM for Facebook ads are $1.72 and $7.34, respectively.
g. 85% of Facebook videos are viewed without sound.

h. Facebook videos that are square receive 35% more views than videos that are landscape.

i. Facebook pages are used by more than 80 million companies.

j. Facebook is used for advertising by 86% of U.S. marketers.

Chapter 5

Facebook Marketing

Facebook marketing is a platform that puts a range of organic and paid advertisements that are highly targeted in front of its huge audience. Facebook is a good platform for business marketing for the reasons listed below:

1. It offers worldwide coverage.
2. It provides highly targeted paid advertisements or promotions.
3. It increases the effectiveness of organic marketing.
4. It enables integrations with other marketing channels

How do Facebook advertisements operate?

Geographically and over time, small businesses have increasingly used it because it operates more simply than search engine advertising. But as with any digital marketing channel, it is more productive for a pro to plan and manage campaigns in Facebook Ads.

Users are specifically targeted by Facebook ads based on their location, demographics, and profile data. Following the creation of your advertisement, you establish a budget and place a bid for each click or each thousand impressions.

The following are factors you should take into account when using Facebook ads:

1. Confide in the effectiveness of Facebook ads for your company.
2. A specific objective is required.
3. Utilize Facebook advertising by doing extensive research on your rivals.
4. Knowing your KPI
5. Build a small, targeted customer base
6. Make rotating advertisements
7. Ensure that the results of your split tests are statistically significant.

Facebook Advertising Abbreviations

➢ KPIs: Key Performance Indicators
➢ CPM: Cost Per Thousand Impressions
➢ CPC: Cost Per Click
➢ PPC: Pay Per Click
➢ PPV: Pay Per View
➢ VTC: View Through Click
➢ CPL: Cost Per Lead

- CPA: Cost Per Acquisition

- CTR: Cost Through Rate

- DSP: Demand Site Platform

- CTA: Call To Action

- RTB: Real Time Bidding

- DMA: Designated Market Area

- IAB: Interactive Advertising Bureau

- ROS: Run of Site

- RON: Run of Network

- CBO: Campaign Budget Optimization

- ROAS: Return on Advertising Spend

- ROI: Return on Investment

- SEM: Search Engine Marketing

- SEO: Search Engine Optimization

- SOV: Share of Voice

Facebook advertising rules

Facebook has adopted guidelines on what kinds of ad content are permitted under its "advertising policy." Each advertisement is examined in light of these guidelines when advertisers place an order. To prevent your ad or your ad account from being disabled, it is advised that you read the Facebook Advertising Policy before running any ads on the social media platform.

Chapter 6

Facebook Ads Hierarchy, Account Setup, and Campaign Objectives.

The following chart should be used by all advertisers to determine which comes first when running Facebook ads.

Steps for creating a Facebook Ad account

Every Facebook account comes with a default ad account

❖ You must first create an ad account before you can run Facebook ads; after that, click on the "Create an account."

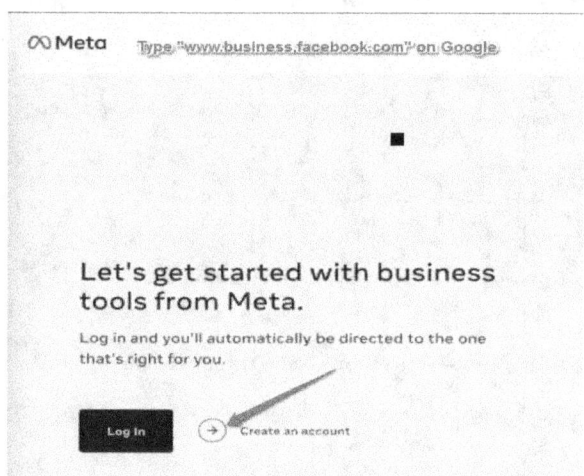

❖ You will see a form that you must complete by entering "Your business and account name," "Your name," and "Your business email address." After that, press the "submit" button.

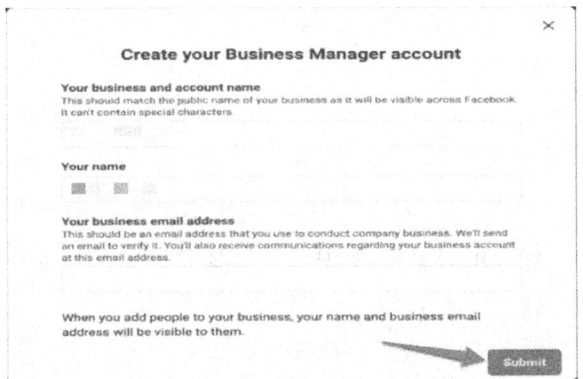

❖ To confirm your registration, sign in to your registered email address, go to your Inbox, and click the link Facebook has sent you. Next, select "Done" from the menu.

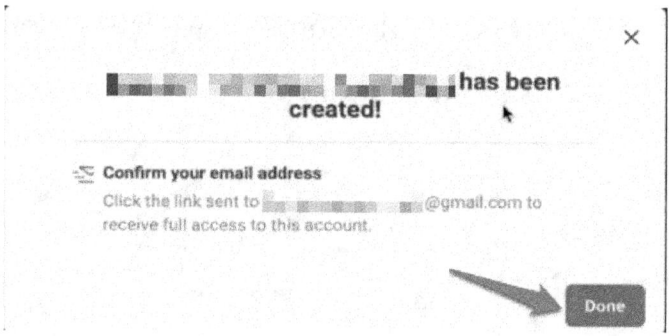

❖ Open your email and click the "Confirm Now" button.

❖ This is how your business manager will appear:

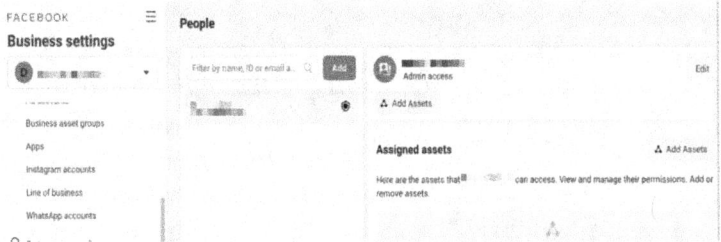

❖ Select "Pages" from the drop-down menu in the Accounts section. The goal is to add your Facebook business page.

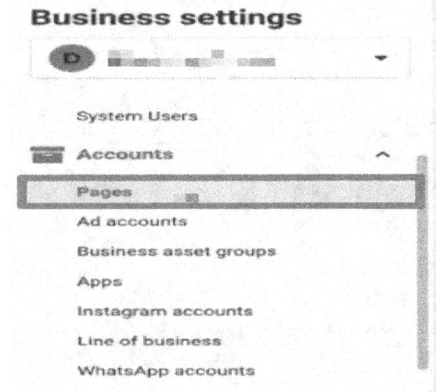

❖ Your Facebook business page can be added. By clicking the "Add" button, select "Create a New Page."

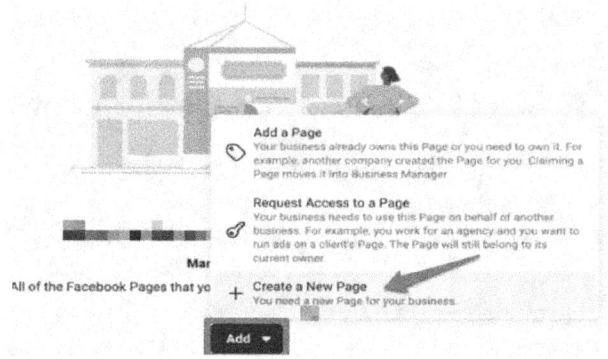

❖ Select a category. I'll pick a "Local Business or Place," for instance.

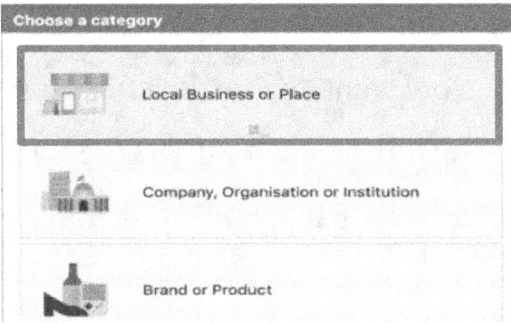

❖ Complete the application for the category you've selected. Click the "Create Page" button after that.

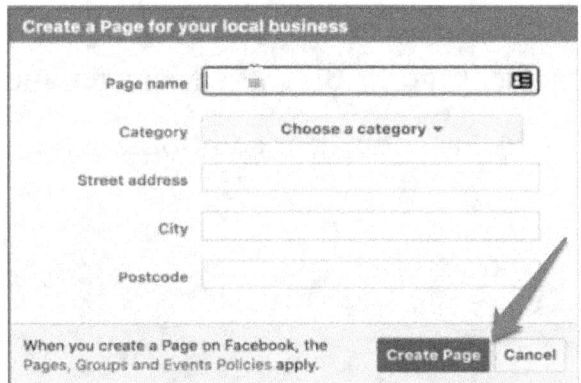

❖ Your business page will be created, and if you want to see it, click "view page" by opening a new tab. There will be settings, a cover page, and so on to be added.

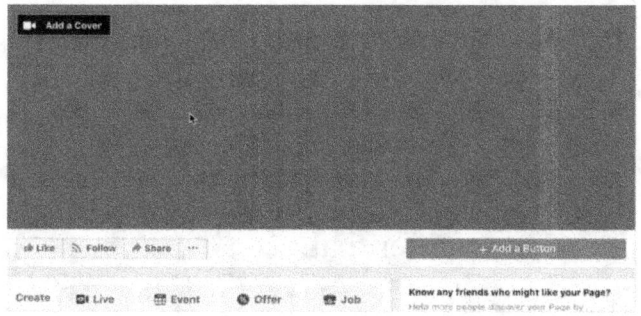

❖ Next, go to Business Manager and choose "Ad account" for additional settings.

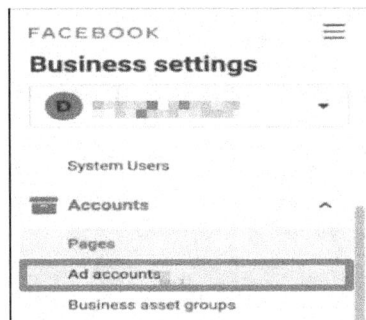

❖ Choose "Create a new ad account" by clicking the "Add" button. Click the "Next" button after completing all the required fields.

❖ Click the "create" button after selecting the goal for your newly created ad account.

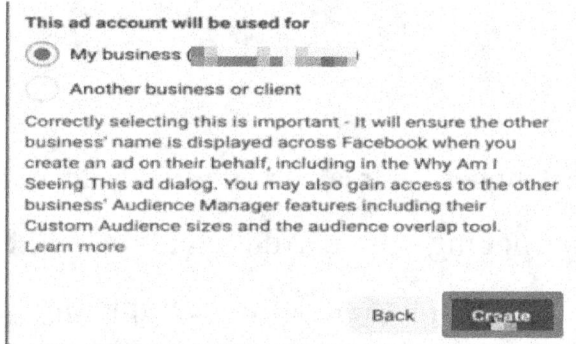

❖ It is requesting authorization to access your advertising account. Turn on the Your Name & Full Control button, then click on the "Assign" button.

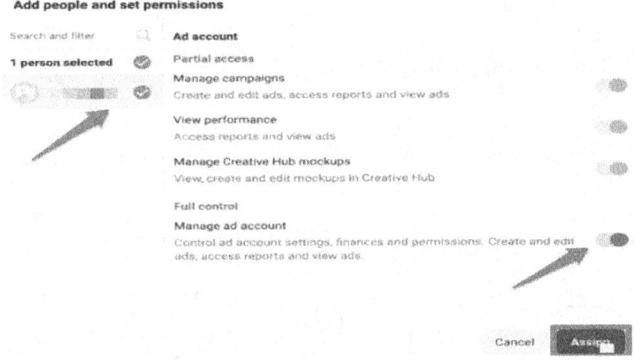

❖ After creating your account, you can add your payment information.

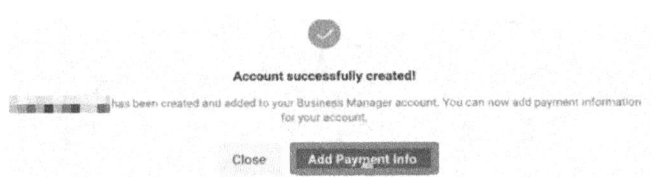

❖ After you've finished with these crucial settings, click "open in Ads Manager" to launch your campaign.

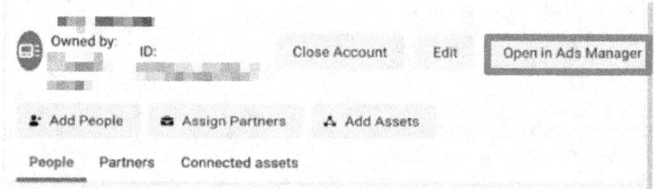

Objectives of Facebook Advertising Campaigns and Their Features

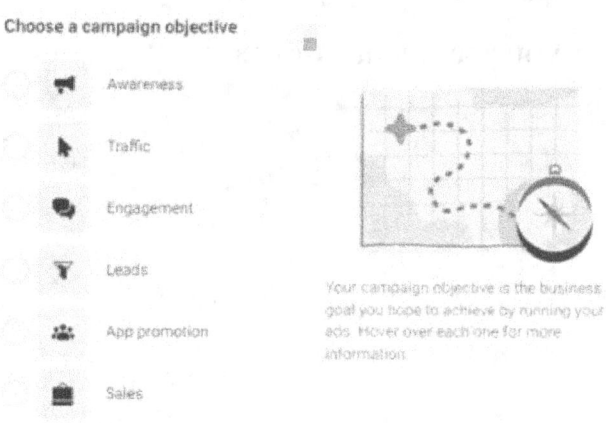

1. Awareness

This applies to promoting your brand, your merchandise, or the services you offer to the public. Large companies that produce sponsored advertisements primarily use it.

This goal will assist you in connecting with the greatest number of people who are most likely to remember your advertisement. For instance, if your company is brand new or has recently changed its name, raising awareness may help prospective customers become more familiar with it.

2. Traffic

This goal will boost traffic to a website of your choice. Direct visitors to a particular place, like your website, app, or store on Facebook or Instagram.

This might encourage traffic to those locations, for instance, if you're running a flash sale in your store or want to direct potential customers to a web page that details your services.

It just involves getting clicks into your ad settings and sending Facebook users to your website or landing page.

3. Engagement

Discover those who are more likely to interact with your company online, send messages, or complete desired actions on your page or ad.

This objective can increase the likelihood that potential customers will start a Messenger conversation if, for example, you want them to do so when they are interested in your products or services.

4. Leads.

This objective can assist you in reaching people who are eager to share their information with you so they can learn more about your company, as in the case of wanting potential customers to sign up for a monthly newsletter.

When you want to expand your business's audiences, this objective is the best choice. Use messages, phone calls, or sign-up forms to gather leads for your business or brand.

5. App Promotion

Get users of mobile devices to download your app or perform a particular action therein. You can design an app promotion campaign, for instance, if you want potential customers to use your app to make a purchase or test out a new feature.

6. Sales

Find those who are most likely to buy your products or services. The sales objective can be used, for instance, if you want to connect with customers who are most likely to make a purchase, perhaps through an online store. You can also make your website more appealing to visitors who add items to their shopping carts.

The effectiveness of this ad objective in tracking any ad manager is crucial for increasing traffic to ads. At this point, a website must have the Meta Pixel installed. It can be used for e-commerce websites, property management, credit card offers, social issues, elections, and politics, among other things. A conversion event and pixel are thus necessary when advertising in this category.

Chapter 7

Facebook Sales or Conversion Ad Campaign

If you want your target audience to visit your website for this type of ad campaign objective, and you want them to do more than just visit—you want them to take action. Therefore, it will be necessary to track and record what they do.

Requirements for Running Sales Ad Campaign

When running a sale campaign and anticipating more clicks and actions from website visitors, the following steps should be taken.

1. Meta Pixel Setup
2. Event Setup

3. Target Location
4. Target Audience, Interest, and Demographic
5. Domain Verification
6. Budget (Daily or Lifetime)
7. Image or Video copy

Installing Facebook Pixel on your website and configuring its events are necessary before you can launch a sales ad campaign.

Sales Ads Campaign Setup with Meta Pixel and Event

I'll define a few terms related to it before I walk you through the procedures and instructions for adding Facebook Pixel to your website and setting up events for the ad campaign.

Meta Pixel

This is a piece of code that you add to your website. It gathers information that enables you to monitor conversions from Facebook ads, optimize ads, create targeted audiences for subsequent ads, and remarket to website visitors who have already taken some sort of action. It enables you to track every action that takes place on your website so that you can retarget everyone who comes to it.

Additionally, it is claimed to be a data-gathering tool that enables you to optimize your Facebook and Instagram ads.

The significance of installing Meta Pixel

1. It boosts the ROI for Facebook advertising.

2. It makes use of Facebook conversion tracking.

3. It creates lookalike audiences

4. Facebook retargeting is utilized.

5. Facebook Ads are optimized for specific actions.

6. It makes use of additional Facebook ad tools and metrics.

Steps for adding Meta Pixel to your WordPress website

You can install the Facebook pixel into your WordPress website by following the instructions below:

❖ On your campaign page, click the three
horizontal lines in the upper left-hand
corner.

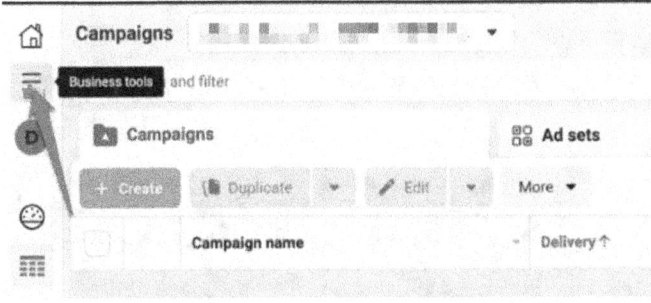

❖ Then, choose "Events Manager."

❖ Click the green-highlighted word "+ Connect data sources" once it has loaded.

❖ Click the "connect" button after selecting "web."

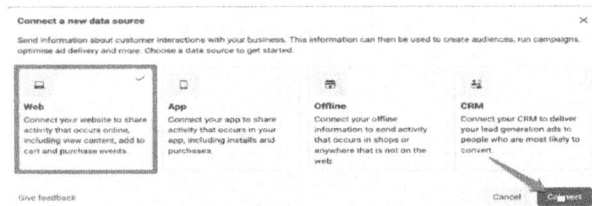

❖ Select "Facebook Pixel" and click on the "connect" button.

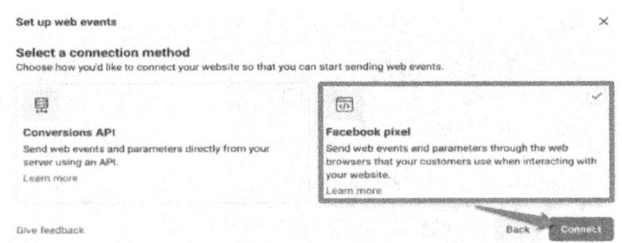

❖ Click "Continue" to view the Facebook pixel's activity on the following page.

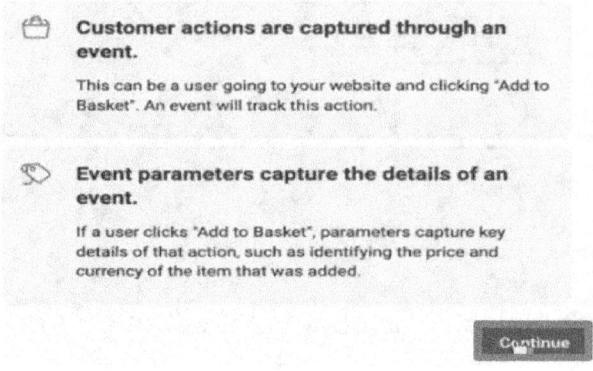

After naming your pixel and adding your website's information to the form, click "Continue."

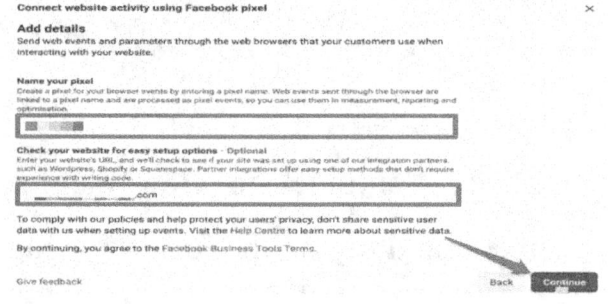

Next, click on the "Continue Pixel Setup." button.

A.G PIXELS

Overview   Test events   Diagnostics   History   Settings

Your pixel hasn't received any activity.
This can happen when the pixel base code isn't installed
correctly on your website. Finish the pixel installation on your
website, including adding events, to start seeing activity.

Continue Pixel Setup

❖ Click "Connect" when Step 5 appears again.

❖ You will have the option of selecting the method of pixel code installation. Click the "install code manually" button after selecting "manually add pixel code to the website."

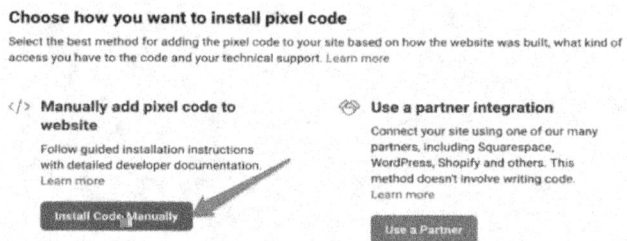

Choose how you want to install pixel code

Select the best method for adding the pixel code to your site based on how the website was built, what kind of access you have to the code and your technical support. Learn more

</> **Manually add pixel code to website**

Follow guided installation instructions with detailed developer documentation. Learn more

Install Code Manually

Use a partner integration

Connect your site using one of our many partners, including Squarespace, WordPress, Shopify and others. This method doesn't involve writing code. Learn more

Use a Partner

❖ Select option 1 and click the green "copy code" button to add the base code to your website. Do this by pasting the code into your website's header section.

Install base code

The pixel code is a snippet of JavaScript that's added to the header section of your website. The pixel has two parts: the base code and the event tags.

① **Copy base code**

Copy the base code below:

```
<!-- Facebook Pixel Code -->
<script>
!function(f,b,e,v,n,t,s)
{if(f.fbq)return;n=f.fbq=function(){n.callMethod?
```

< —/>

Copy code

❖ You'll be adding this JavaScript snippet to your WordPress website. Log in to your WordPress website. Choose "Plugins" from the list of three options that appears at the bottom of your dashboard, then click "Add New."

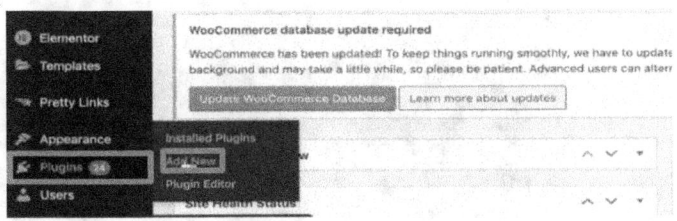

❖ Type "tracking code manager" into the keyword search field. The "Install Now" and "Activate" buttons should be clicked.

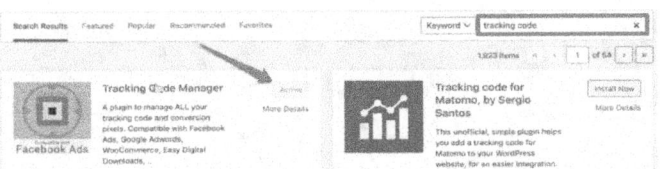

❖ Click on "tracking code manager" in the
   "settings" section of your WordPress
   dashboard to access the plugin you just
   added

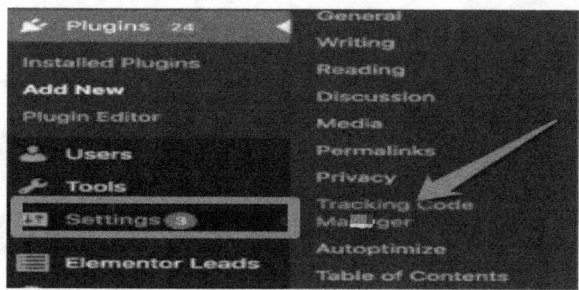

❖ There are already a few tracking codes
   installed; simply click on the "Add new
   Tracking Code" button.

❖ Give it a name, like FACEBOOK ADS, and then paste the copied snippet of code into the box provided.

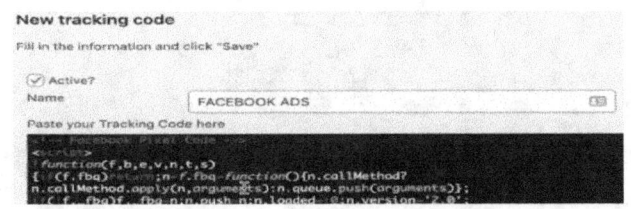

❖ After pasting the code, scroll down to ensure that it appears on all devices and is positioned before the header section.

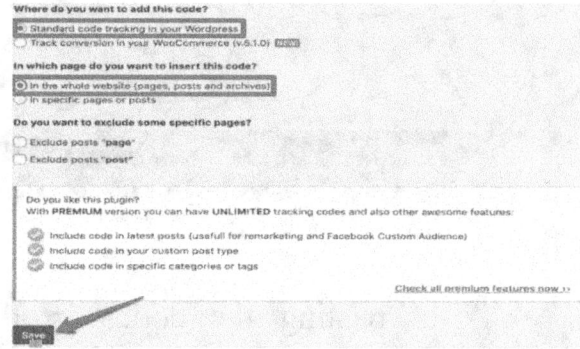

| Position inside the code | Before </HEAD> | ▾ |
| Show only on device | × [All] | |

❖ Subsequently choose "In the whole website (pages, posts, and archives)" under "Standard code tracking in your WordPress." Then scroll down and click on the "Save." button.

Where do you want to add this code?
◉ Standard code tracking in your Wordpress
○ Track conversion in your WooCommerce (v.5.1.0) [NEW]

In which page do you want to insert this code?
◉ In the whole website (pages, posts and archives)
○ In specific pages or posts

Do you want to exclude some specific pages?
○ Exclude posts "page"
○ Exclude posts "post"

Do you like this plugin?
With PREMIUM version you can have UNLIMITED tracking codes and also other awesome features:
- Include code in latest posts (usefull for remarketing and Facebook Custom Audience)
- Include code in your custom post type
- Include code in specific categories or tags

Check all premium features now >>

Save

❖ The tracking code you added will be verified for you.

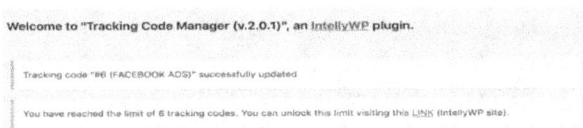

❖ Return to Facebook Business Manager. You've finished the first two steps; the final step of the settings is to turn on the "Automatic advance matching" button and then click "Add event code." button.

Automatic advanced matching

Use information that your customers have already provided to your business, such as their email addresses or phone numbers, to match your website's visitors to people who are on Facebook. This can help you attribute more conversions to your ads on Facebook and reach more people through remarketing campaigns. Learn More

⬤ Turn on automatic advanced matching

Verify the customer information that you want to send.

⬤ Email address   ⬤ Gender   ⬤ Town/city, county/region, postal code and country

⬤ First name and surname ⬤ Phone number   ⬤ Date of birth

⬤ External ID

This information will be hashed to better protect user privacy before it is sent to Facebook. Sensitive information, such as financial, health and government ID data, will not be sent. Learn More

I'll go over a few procedures for setting up an event when explaining a standard event. You can check to see if the pixel code has been added to or is already present on your website.

❖ The Facebook Pixel Helper extension needs to be downloaded and added to your Chrome browser. Once you have finished installing Chrome on your computer and have entered your website's URL into Google, it will appear as shown below. Additionally, it will display the event you added along with your Facebook Pixel ID and other data that corresponds to your Ad Manager.

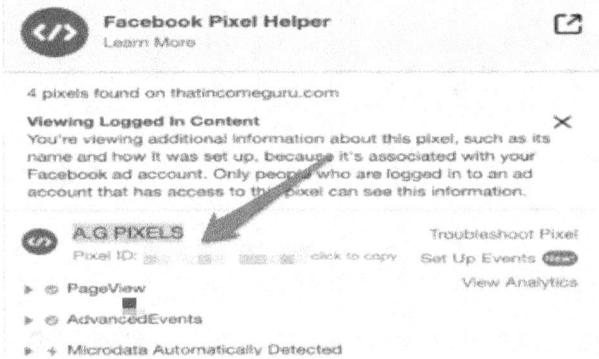

Integration

This refers to the platform you use to build your website, so you can quickly link your most recent work to it. Examples include customer management system (CMS) platforms like Woocommerce, Shopify, Magento, Joomla, Kajabi, Wix, WordPress, and so on. The Facebook Pixel must be copied and installed to use any of the aforementioned platforms.

Audience

When running Facebook ads, we focus on two categories of audience:

1. Custom Audience

These are people you are retargeting who have interacted with your website or expressed interest in your company or product. It is primarily employed in retargeting ad campaigns.

2. Lookalike Audience

These are new people who share the same interests as the custom audience you have created, but they are not familiar with your brand.

Note: *Unless your target audiences are completely different or your business is completely different, you only need to set up one pixel and install it on your ad account.*

Types of Event

The behavior of website visitors is tracked using an event setup tool.

1. Standard Event

This is an event that Facebook uses to ascertain the specific action users are taking in relation to an ad account, a Facebook page, an Instagram page, or your website. Two methods exist for adding the Facebook Pixel event code:

a. Facebook Event Setup Tool (Recommended)

b. Manually add event code: The best choice is to use this if you want to send someone to your thank-you page or any other kind of alternative destination.

Add to cart, Schedule, Purchase, Complete Registration, Customize Product, Find Location, Lead, Search, Submit Application, View content, and other examples of standard events. Therefore, this event type is frequently used. The most important events to track are Email Opt-In, Lead, and View content.

The most crucial events to track if you manage an e-commerce website are Add to cart, Abandon cart, Add Payment Info, Purchase, and Lead.

How to set up a Standard event

You must have these two things available to start setting up a standard event.

a. Chrome browser
b. Installing Facebook Pixel Helper on your Chrome extension is required.

The Steps are as follows:

❖ Go to Business Settings on your Ads Manager dashboard and select "Event Manager.

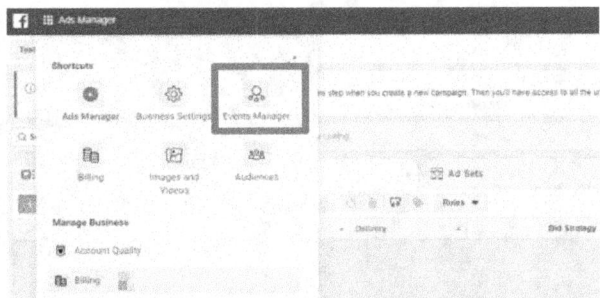

❖ Choose the created pixel by clicking on the "+ Connect data sources" word that is highlighted in green. After that, click "Add Event"

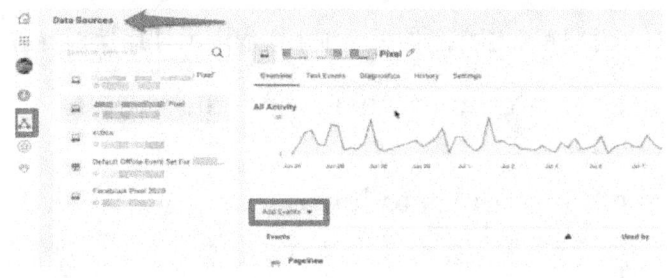

❖ Choose "From the Pixel" from the list of three options.

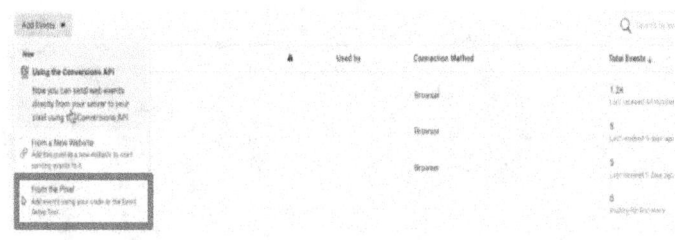

❖ The "Launch Event Setup Tool" button should be clicked.

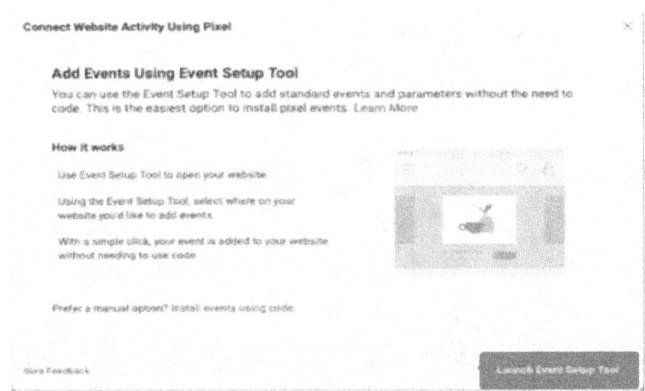

❖ Enter the URL of the website you want to use to track events. After that, click on the "open website" button.

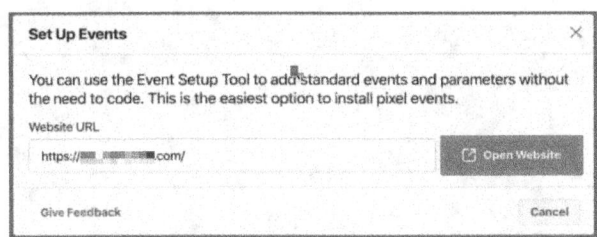

❖ There are two choices available once your website has loaded. You can either use the "Track New Button" or "Track a URL." In this instance, we'll choose "Track New Button."

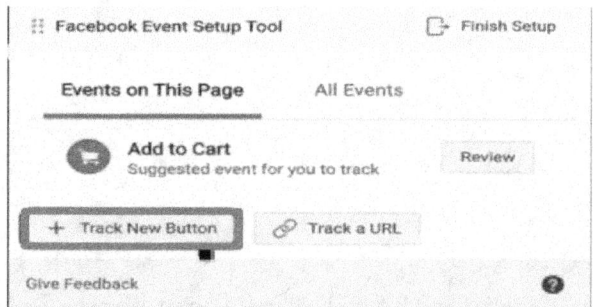

❖ The "Get Instant Access" button on my website is the one I'll be tracking. I'll click on it.

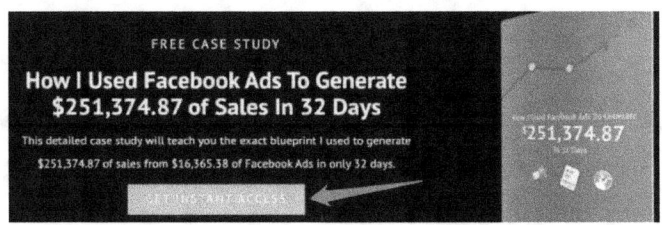

❖ Choose the event type you want to track. I'll select "view content" by toggling on the button, and then "confirm."

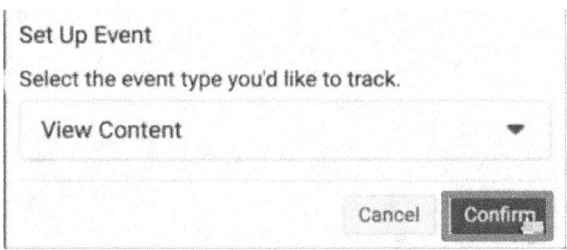

❖ You can see that it has been set up.

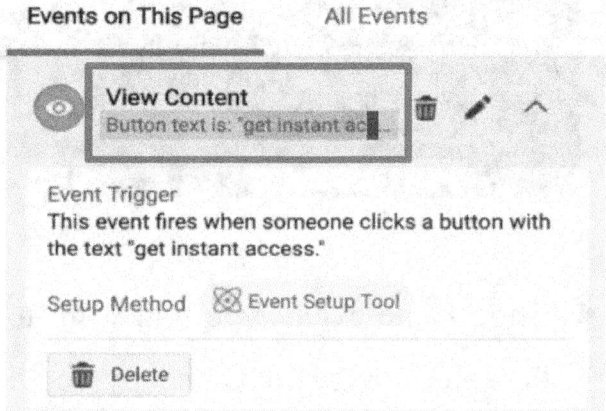

❖ Next, press the "Finish setup" and the "Finish" buttons.

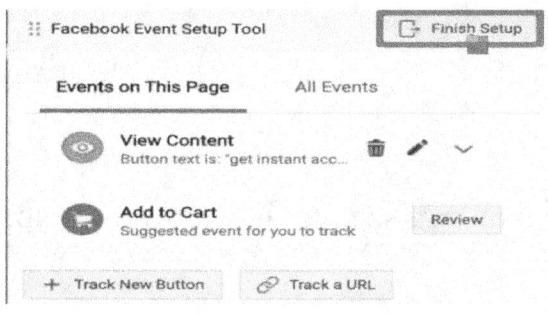

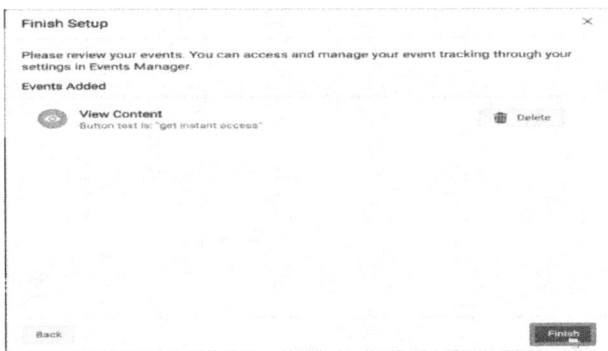

❖ The event setting is complete. Next, click on the "Test Events" button.

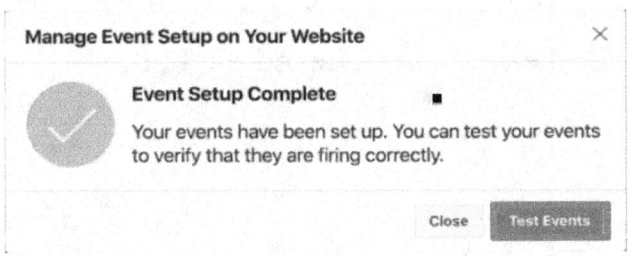

❖ To verify, re-enter the URL of your website.

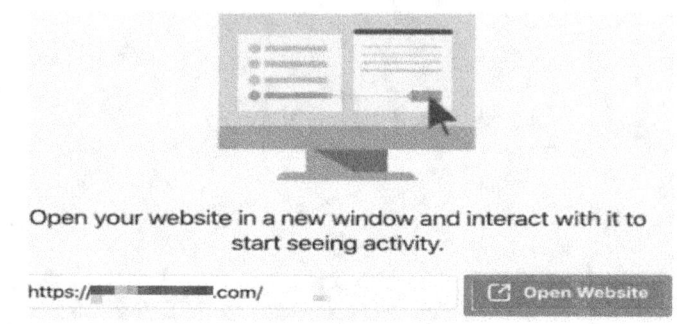

Open your website in a new window and interact with it to
start seeing activity.

https://███████████.com/   [⌐] Open Website

❖ Fill out the required field (or whatever it
may be in your case) after clicking the
"Get Instant Access" button we tracked. I
filled in the form as it was displayed
below, and I clicked the button.

Free Case Study

How I Used Facebook Ads To
Generate $251,374.87 of
Sales In 32 Days

This detailed case study will
teach you the exact blueprint I
used to generate $251,374.87 of
sales from $16,365.38 of
Facebook Ads in only 32 days.

Simply enter your first name and email for instant
access.

First Name

Email Address

GET INSTANT ACCESS +

100% Spam Free Zone. Unsubscribe Anytime.

❖ All of your Ad Manager information, including the new event you've set up, will be displayed when you click Facebook Pixel Helper in the top-right corner of your Chrome browser. that is, "view content"

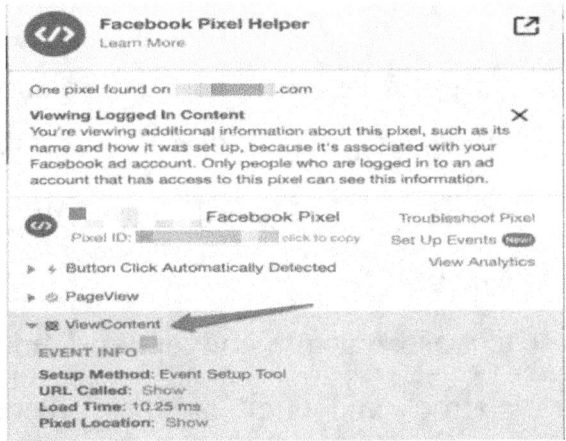

2. Custom Event

This is a self-defined event that occurs when someone visits your particular page, attends your webinar, or browses your product page. You define it based on their digital behaviors.

3. Custom Conversion

You'll use the URL in this option; for instance, if someone visits your thank-you page, you'll use your website's URL to track their behavior.

Simple steps for setting up custom conversion

❖ Go to Business Settings on your Ads Manager dashboard and select "Event Manager."

❖ Choose "custom conversions" under "Data source" and click on the "create custom conversions" button.

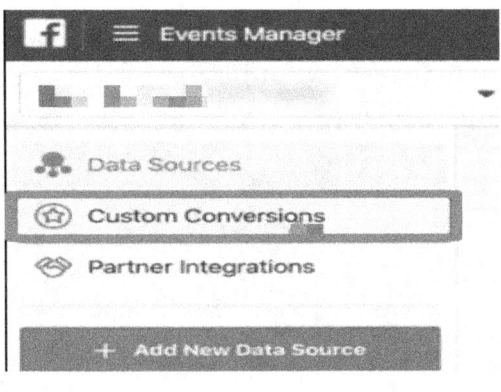

❖ Your website's URL must include the destination URL of the website page you want to visit under "website events," which I've highlighted with an arrow.

You should do this because you want to collect leads from every possible variation of your URL. Therefore, selecting "contains" is the best option.

❖ Lastly, enter the name, description, category, and value. Let the category of your custom conversion reflect the goal of your business. then click on the "create" button.

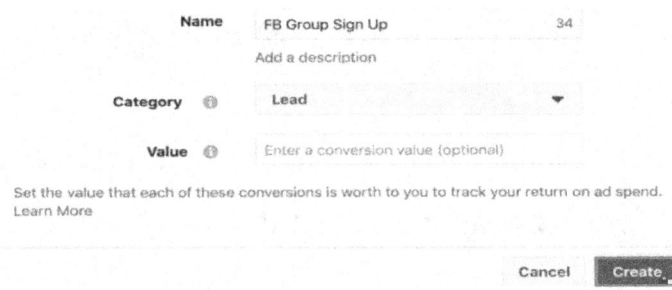

Now that you are familiar with some terminology associated with setting up a conversion ad campaign. It's crucial to understand every step I just described before you launch your conversion campaign with Facebook Ads.

How to Set up Facebook Ads with Sales campaign

An ad campaign on Facebook is set up in three steps. These are campaigns, ad sets, and ads. I will use "real estate" as a niche for this book, with an annex illustration to step-by-step explain this.

❖ Click the green "+create" button on your Ads Manager dashboard.

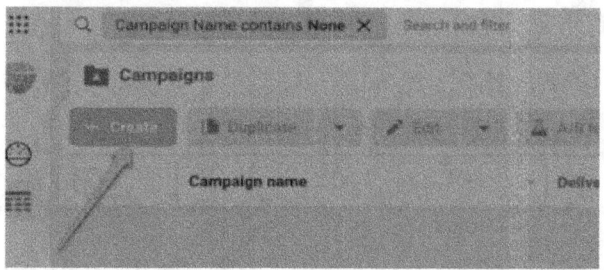

❖ Select the "Sales" objective and click on the "Continue" button at the campaign level.

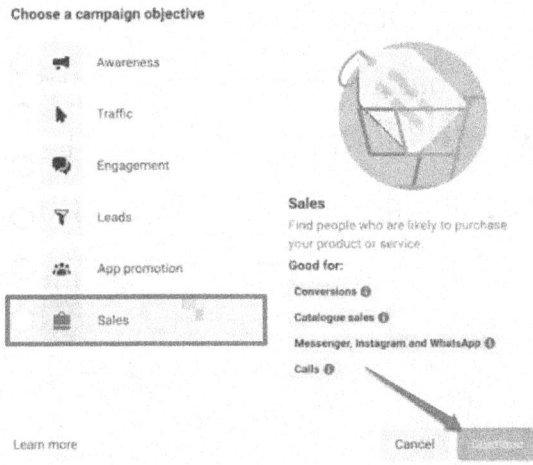

Choose a campaign objective

- Awareness
- Traffic
- Engagement
- Leads
- App promotion
- Sales

Sales
Find people who are likely to purchase your product or service.
Good for:
Conversions
Catalogue sales
Messenger, Instagram and WhatsApp
Calls

Learn more   Cancel

❖ Next, choose any campaign name that makes sense to you. I chose "webinar conversions." Turn off special Ad categories.

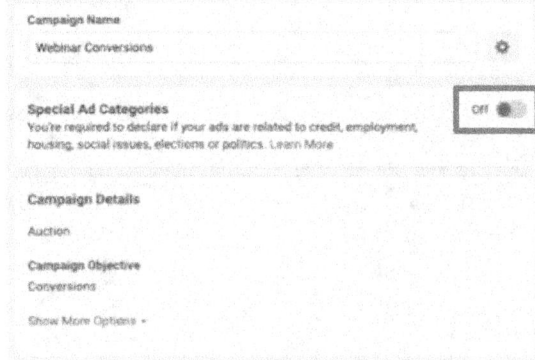

Campaign Name

Webinar Conversions

Special Ad Categories
You're required to declare if your ads are related to credit, employment, housing, social issues, elections or politics. Learn More   Off

Campaign Details
Auction

Campaign Objective
Conversions

Show More Options ▾

❖ You can conduct an A/B test if you want to, but this book will not cover it.

❖ The next option is CBO, Leave it Off," and you can set your budget at the Ad Sets level. To continue, click on the "Next" button.

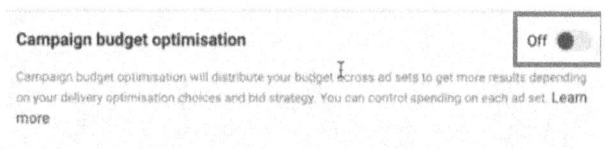

❖ At the Ad Sets level, choose "website" as the Conversion Event Location and give it a name.

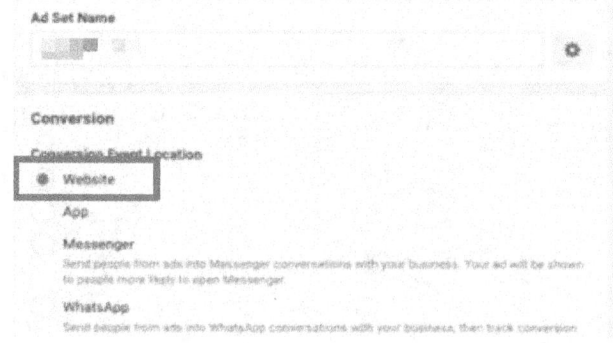

❖ Choose the Pixel and Conversion event you created. It is active, as indicated by the green color. To indicate that it is in active mode, it must be green.

❖ The next option is dynamic creative; if you enable it, it will let you create your ad with multiple headlines, images, and pieces of copy when you move on to the following step, and Facebook will test and optimize them automatically. It's a good option if you're running an A/B test and don't want to go through additional steps; however, you'll need to toggle on the "dynamic creative" button. However, I turned it off for the sake of simplicity.

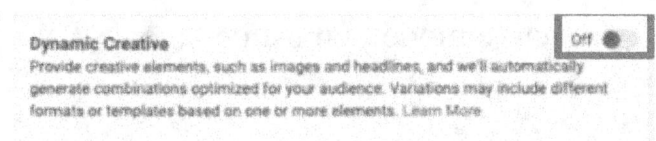

❖ Budget and schedule come next.

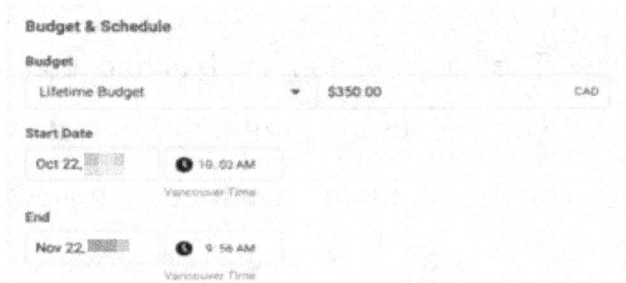

➢ Daily Budget: This indicates that you spend a certain amount each day.

➢ Lifetime Budget: This indicates that you're setting a budget based on a time frame and telling Facebook not to go over that total during your campaign.

❖ The audience section comes next. You can "use saved audiences" if you've previously created them and want to use them. You can "create a new audience"

➢ Audiences: Before launching your advertising campaign, you are advised to conduct audience research. Select Audience Insights from the list of business tools. To see your exact preference, enter your location, age range, and interest.

➢ Location: Canada and the United States are my two targeted locations.

➢ Detailed Targeting: You can narrow your audiences and target people based on their demographics, interests, or behaviors. Then, you might want to select "Save this Audience." When you save it, it turns into a custom audience that you can retarget when you run another ad campaign.

❖ Placements come next. Your advertisement will essentially appear here on social media. Keep it set to "Automatic Placements" so Facebook can perfect your ad. You should skip "Optimization and Delivery."

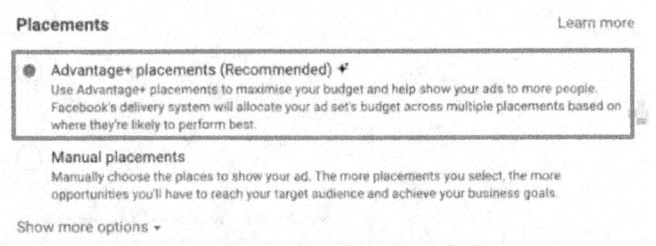

❖ At the Ad level, select your Facebook page and give your ad a name. if it had already been chosen. It's ok.

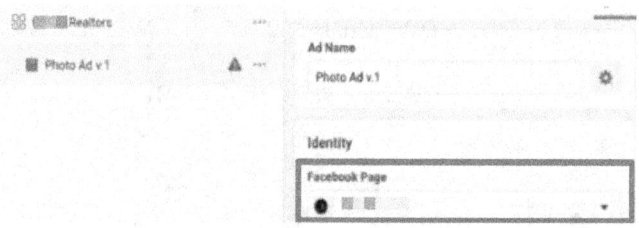

❖ Next, in the ad setup, I'll use the "single image video" format, and when my target audiences click on it, they'll be taken to my website. With CTA, a carousel can be used for a variety of products.

Ad Setup

Create Ad ▾

Format
Choose how you'd like to structure your ad.

● Single Image or Video
One image or video, or a slideshow with multiple images

○ Carousel
2 or more scrollable images or videos

○ Collection
Group of items that opens into a fullscreen mobile experience

Fullscreen Mobile Experience

Add an Instant Experience

Add a Playable Source File

❖ Next, move on to the section for the "Ad creative".

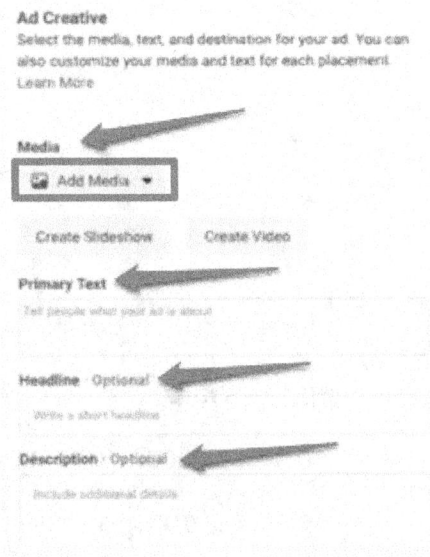

➢ Add Media: You can select a ready-made image or you design it from scratch

➢ Primary Text: It adheres to these three procedures.

★ Hook line or Key: Make use of an intriguing subject. For instance, *"Where is my order?" "Pamper your pouch, they deserve it," "How to generate over 150 leads per month on total autopilot,"* and *"Avoid wasting time on repetitive tasks."* You can also add an emoji icon to your hook when appropriate.

★ Product description and Solution: Your campaign's goal or objective must be specified. For instance, *"I see so many agents wasting their valuable time on...", "25% off dog treats", "trusted by 4000+ eCommerce stores,"* and add an emoji icon to your details.

★ Call-to-Action: For instance, *click here to learn more about our free master class*.

All of the aforementioned elements must be present in your primary text.

➤ Headlines: Use a captivating word, for example: "how to generate 150+ leads per month on autopilot."

➤ Destination: You will choose "website" and enter the address of your website.

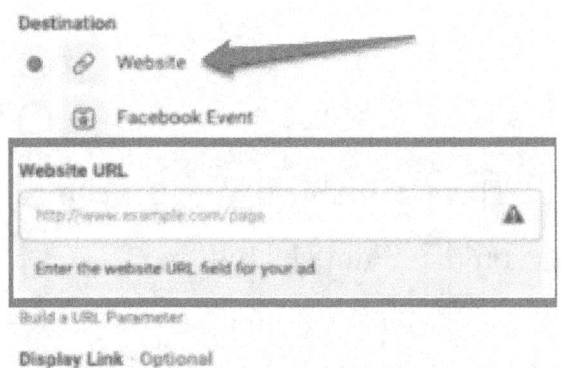

➤ Call-to-Action: Choose the most effective CTA for your ad campaign and ad copy.

❖ The pixel and event you have created can be found under "Tracking" when you scroll down.

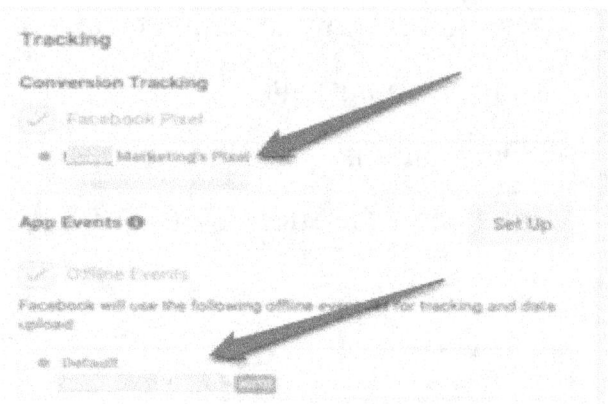

Then, to publish your ad campaign, click on the "Publish" button.

Facebook Ads Copy, Ads Sample, and Cover Page

Facebook ad copy is the expression of the hook; it is the justification for why your audience should take the action you are requesting. Ad copy is where you "meet them in the conversation that's already going on in their mind," whether you're asking them to watch a video or opt-in to a lead magnet.

Analyzing the ad copy of your competitors is crucial to staying ahead of them. To get ad copy samples for all niches, visit the Facebook Library, where varieties of the copy are available and are being categorized based on your niche.

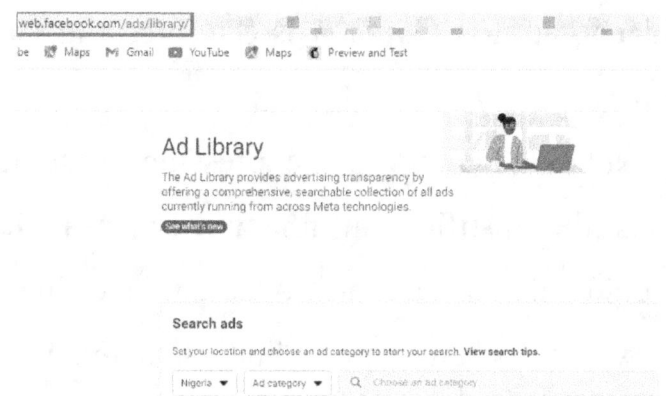

After modifying pertinent ad copy for your campaign, the purpose of doing this is to stand out among your competitors.

Bigspy will help you acquire Facebook ad samples with primary text that targets various niches. Visit the website and select a plan for your sample ad.

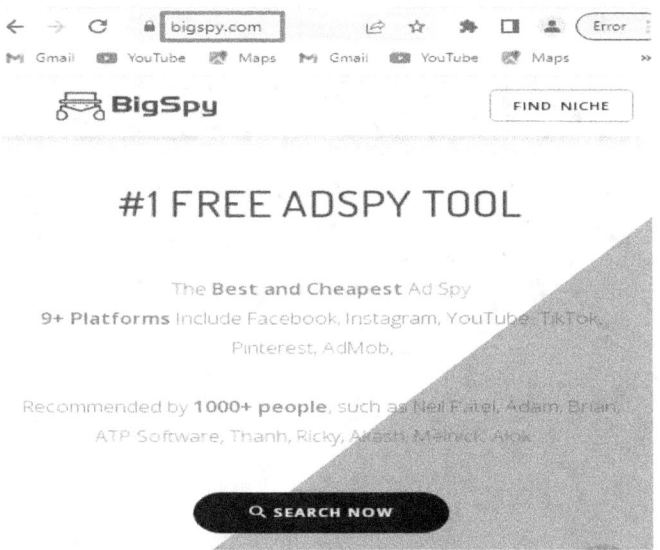

Last but not least, the Facebook ad's cover page is the first thing viewers will see when they see your ad, so it's critical to make the best first impression and grab their attention. The minimum dimensions for the Facebook cover page as of 2022 were 400 by 150 pixels.

The website to visit is "Placeit" in order to get a pertinent cover page for your advertisement.

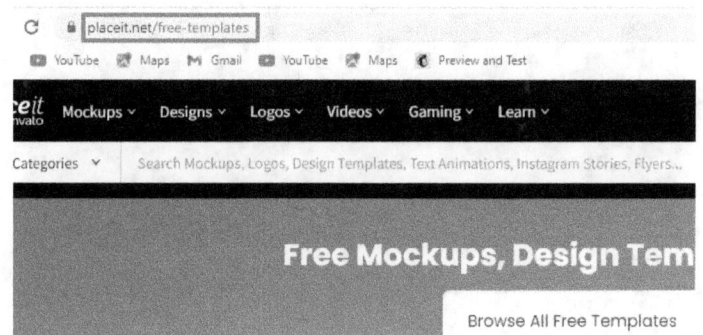

Chapter 8

Retargeting Ad Campaign

Retargeting is the practice of putting your advertising campaign in front of a specific group of people who have previously shown interest in your product or service. Remarketing is another name for Retargeting.

When you are retargeting your audience, you require a minimum of 100 people; if you have fewer than 100 people, your ad will not run. When your audience is less than or equal to 100 people, don't bother with retargeting. Retargeting won't be successful until you have thousands of people to work with.

How to retarget your Facebook ad campaign in different ways.

❖ Click the green "+create" button on your Ads Manager dashboard.

❖ At the Campaign level, select "conversion" for the campaign's objective and press "continue"

❖ Go directly to the "Adset" level since that is where you will perform Retargeting. Go to the audience section, then click "Create New." and choose "Custom Audience" from the drop-down menu.

❖ You can retarget your audience in a variety of ways, including using your website, customer list, videos, lead forms, events, Facebook Pages, shopping, etc.

Create a Custom Audience

Use your sources

🌐 Website	👥 Customer list
📱 App activity	🏃 Offline activity

Use Facebook sources

▶ Video	📷 Instagram account
📝 Lead form	📅 Events
Instant Experience	🏳 Facebook Page
🛒 Shopping	On-Facebook Listings

❖ Select your pixel after clicking on the website. Adding or excluding people is another option. then give your audience a name.

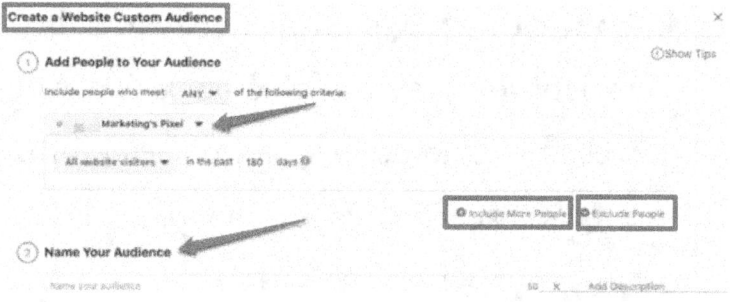

➢ Website Traffic: If you select this as an option in Step 5 above (Website), Facebook Pixel must be installed. There is a maximum of 180 days that you can select.

❖ You have the option to add fields to your customer list. Additionally, you can import your list from Mailchimp's email marketing tool.

Create an Audience From a Customer List

Prepare Your Customer List

Your customer list is a CSV or TXT file that contains information used to build your audience. Identifiers in your customer list are used to match with Facebook users. The more identifiers you provide, the better the match rate.

Include at least one main identifier

Email | Phone Number | Mobile Advertiser ID | Facebook App User ID
Facebook Page User ID | First Name | Last Name

Include more identifiers

City | State/Province | Country | ZIP/Postal Code | Date of Birth
Year of Birth | Gender | Age

Add value information to create a value-based lookalike

Customer Value

⬇ Download List Template
🔗 See Formatting Guidelines
📷 Import From Mailchimp

➢ Customer List: If this is the option that was chosen in step 6, you can just upload the list of people on Facebook and run ads to them. It needs to be uploaded based on specific fields like first name, last name, gender, country, postal code, etc. The more information you give on Facebook, the better they're going to match the information you've presented.

❖ When you select an Instagram account as an option, choose your Instagram page.

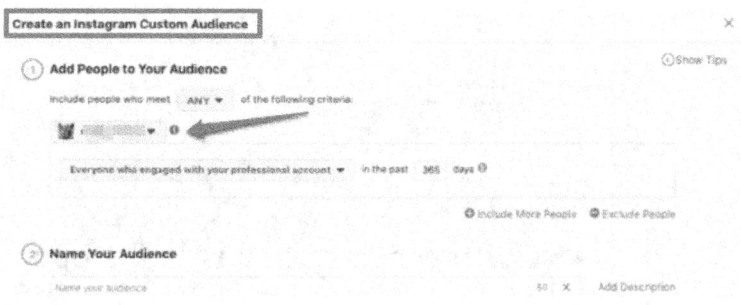

➢ Instagram Account: Those who interacted with your professional account over the previous 365 days.

❖ It functions similarly to an Instagram account when you choose a Facebook Page.

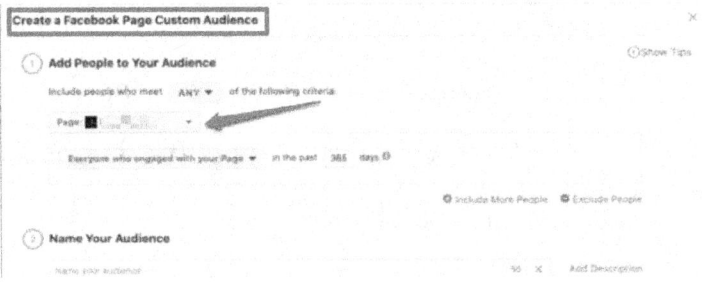

> Facebook Page: Those who interacted with your page over the previous 365 days.

❖ On the Facebook page, you can select an event.

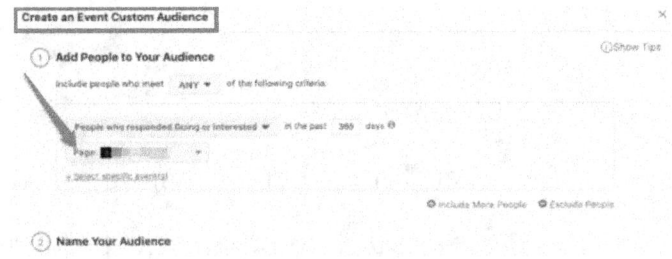

➢ Event: These are people that have attended an event you created in the last 365 days. A specific event will then be chosen.

❖ This retargeting option is necessary if you are running a lead generation campaign because it asks your audience to fill out and submit important information.

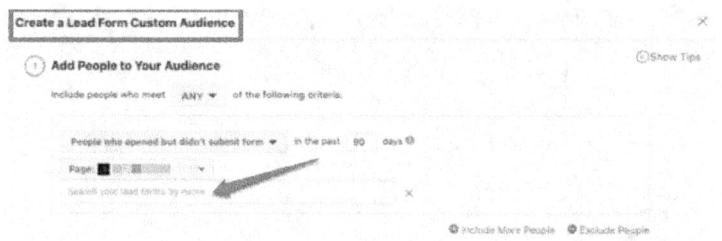

➢ Lead Form: People who opened the form but did not submit it will need to choose this option. 90 days is the maximum allowed time for this.

❖ You can select your preferred video engagement option from the previous 365 days.

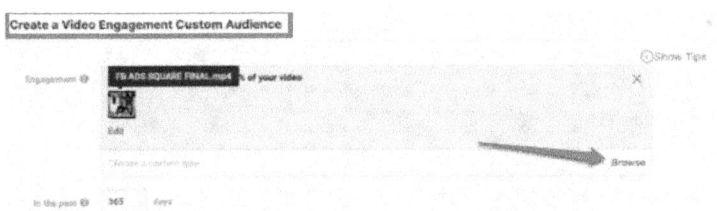

➢ Video Engagement: Based on their interactions in previous years, you can retarget viewers of some of your videos, and the video is segmented based on duration. You may run advertisements for this group of people using a video ad or

Facebook   posted   video.
Additionally, more than one video
can be chosen.

Chapter 9

Facebook Ad Campaign Optimization

Facebook Ad Optimization is a method of increasing the effectiveness of ads that have already been running and keeping track of their performance data. It also describes the process of developing ads that are pertinent to the viewers of your ads and the process of refining these ads using information obtained from A/B tests and user testing.

Ways to optimize Facebook Ad

1. Through Age Groups

The best-performing age groups should receive your budget's attention first. Performing a split on the adset level will be a very good option if you have a large enough audience with a variety of age groups. Do extensive research on Facebook Audience Insights for age targeting.

2. Through Gender

You should only leave one gender if you notice that either men or women are purchasing more of your products.

3. Through Country or Region

Don't start your optimization process by region (such as California). It is acceptable to optimize if you are using the same adset to target several different countries.

4. Through Ad Placement

Facebook offers various ad placement options, including:

   a. Mobile News Feed

   b. Desktop News Feed

c. Instagram

d. Audience Network, and more.

Wait 5-7 days before optimizing your placements, such as Mobile News Feed.

5. Through Budget

Increase your budget by 30–40%, but do not increase it further; wait at least five days before making any further changes.

Misconceptions About Facebook Ads

Most Facebook Ads runners have the following false assumptions:

1. After publishing, Facebook ads immediately begin to run.
2. Good advertisements run forever.
3. Your audience is better known on Facebook.

4. Laser-targeted audiences are necessary (Narrow Audience).

5. You'll generate immediate sales.

How to recover your blocked Facebook Ad Account

⊘ **Ad Account Disabled**

This ad account, its ads and some of its advertising assets are disabled. You can't use it to run ads.

If Facebook disables your Facebook Ad account, it is difficult to get it back, and it could be because you have broken one of their explicit advertising policies. Before launching your advertising campaign, it is advisable to review their terms and conditions.

You can speak with their Support or Business help about this matter. Then, you will be taken to your Messenger chat page with their business support to discuss your case after selecting one or all of the aforementioned protocols and following the proper procedure through the Facebook link that slashes the protocols mentioned.

You will be informed once the issue has been resolved, and they will open a ticket for you and send you to their internal team to investigate any potential causes.

PART C

INSTAGRAM

ADVERTISEMENTS

Chapter 10

Introduction

Instagram advertisements are a feature of Instagram's social network that lets businesses run display ads that specifically target Instagram users. A brand must have a Facebook page and access to an Instagram business profile to use Instagram advertising. After setting everything up, brands can use a variety of ad formats, including photo, carousel, slideshow, video, and story ads.

The custom audiences that are created within the Facebook advertising platform can then be targeted with these ads. Due to the platform's optimization for online shopping, Instagram advertisements are thought to be very effective, especially for businesses involved in the eCommerce sector.

Information Regarding Instagram Advertisements.

The realities of Instagram advertising are listed below:

1. According to 73% of American young adults, Instagram is the best platform for brands to inform them about new products or promotions.
2. As of January 2020, there were more than 1 billion active monthly users.
3. 500+ Million users of Instagram stories each day.
4. Potential advertising reach of 849,3 Million.

5. Shopping posts receive monthly engagement from more than 130 million users.

6. 89% of the time, ads with stories that highlight the CTA button produce better results.

7. After seeing an Instagram advertisement for a brand, 50% of users are more interested in it.

8. In comparison to other well-known social media platforms, 53% of Instagram users follow their favorite brands, and Instagram has 84 times more brand engagement than Twitter, 54 times more than Pinterest, and 10 times more than Facebook.

9. 90% of the "Top 100 Global Brands" use Instagram; 36% of B2C brands and 13%

of B2B brands view Instagram as critical to their marketing strategies.

Requirements for Instagram Ads

The following prerequisites must be met before you can run advertisements on Instagram:

a. Facebook Account.

b. Facebook Business Page.

c. Instagram Business Profile connected to your Facebook Business Page.

d. Facebook Ad Account.

e. Your Budget for the Ads.

Chapter 11

Methods of Connecting Instagram Account and Types of Instagram Advertisements.

You can link your Instagram and Facebook business accounts using two different methods.

1. **Direct Connection through Meta Business account.**
   ❖ On your Facebook business page, go to the "Manage page" and click the "settings" button.

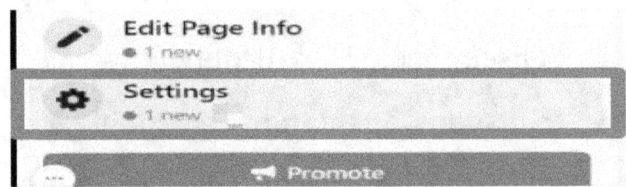

❖ Next, select "Instagram" from the "Page settings" menu by scrolling down to the page's left-hand corner.

❖ After selecting "Instagram" from the page settings menu, you can connect your Instagram account to your Facebook business page. Then reload the page, and "Disconnected" will appear which shows that your Instagram Account has been connected to your Facebook page.

You can launch your Instagram Ads campaign once you've linked your Facebook account to your Instagram account.

2. By Visiting your Instagram Page.

❖ Click the "Edit Profile" button on your dashboard after logging into your Instagram account.

❖ Next, click on the "Switch to Professional Account" button in the bottom left corner of the page.

❖ There will be a page with two options between "Creator" and "Business." After selecting "Business," press the "Next" button.

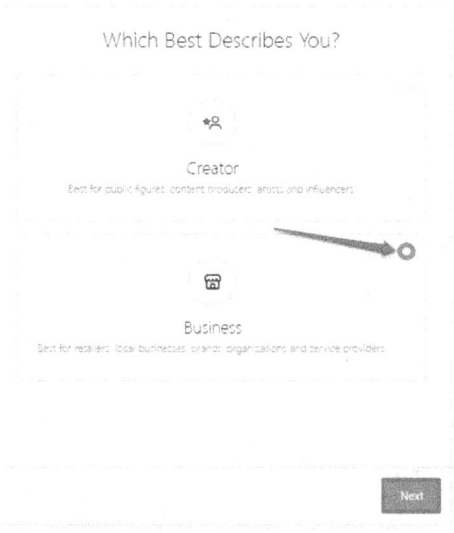

❖ You will be taken to a page with the option you chose for business details; click "Next" once more.

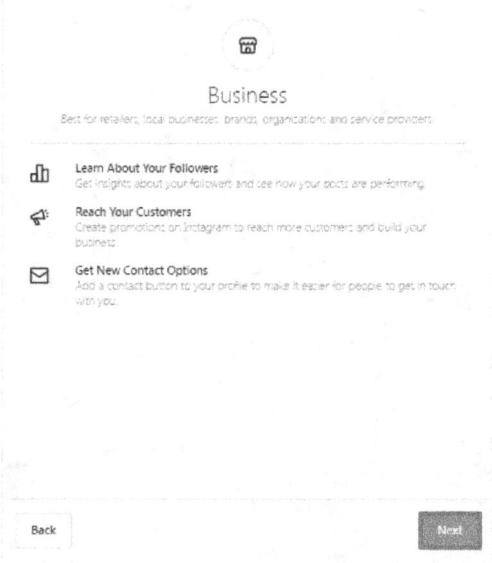

Business

Best for retailers, local businesses, brands, organizations and service providers.

Learn About Your Followers
Get insights about your followers and see how your posts are performing.

Reach Your Customers
Create promotions on Instagram to reach more customers and build your business.

Get New Contact Options
Add a contact button to your profile to make it easier for people to get in touch with you.

Back   Next

❖ Pick a category that best fits the description of your work. I'll choose "Product or Service" and then click on the "Done" button.

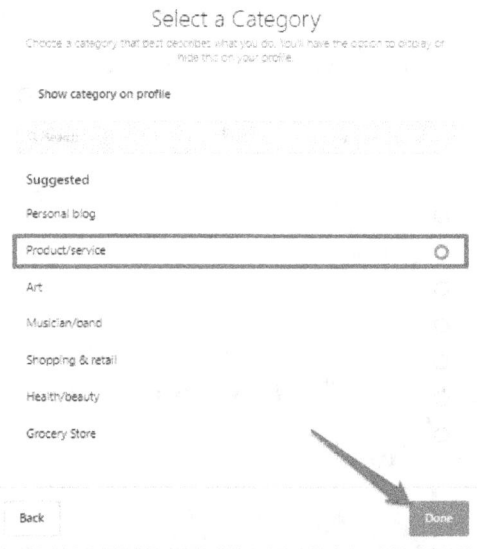

❖ Once you've finished, you'll notice that it has been changed from Personal Account to Professional Account.

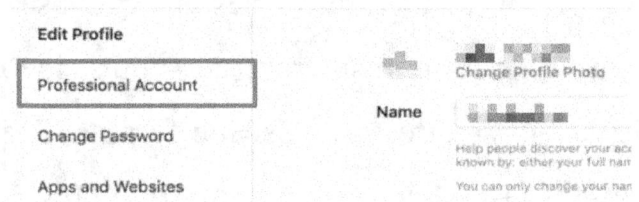

It might already be linked to another Facebook business page if you're trying to connect it but it's not working. It must be disconnected from the previous Facebook page and reconnected to the desired new page.

Instagram Advertisement Types, Formats, and Duration

1. Images

Your Instagram ad may display your image in a square, landscape, or vertical format if you only use one image.

2. Video

Except for Instagram stories, if you use video creative in your Instagram ad, your video may display in square or landscape format. The time frame is always in the range of 30 to 60 seconds.

3. Creative or Carousel

Your Instagram ad will display on feeds and stories in either a square or vertical format if the carousel format is used for the creative.

4. Instagram Stories

While I will advise you to use a full-screen vertical asset in story ads, this format can support the same media you use in other placements. You can upload a single photo or a 120-second video with an aspect ratio of 9:16 or 16:9 to 4:5 for Stories ads that support photo and video feed placement.

Consequently, 10- to 15-second videos are suggested for this kind.

5. IGTV

While I will advise using a full-screen vertical asset for IGTV advertisements, this format can support all video creatives for up to 15 seconds with an aspect ratio of 16:9, 1:1, 4:5, or 9:16.

6. Reels

Reel ads can only be used with full-screen vertical assets.

Therefore, the process for creating Facebook Ads and Instagram Ads is the same; the only differences are in the creative, layout, and placement of the Ads after setting up an Ads campaign.

I'll go into more detail about a traffic ad campaign using Instagram in the following chapter.

Chapter 12

Instagram Traffic Ad Campaign.

For this type of ad campaign objective, you want your target audience to visit your website and you make a record of the number of clicks.

Steps on how to set up Instagram Ads with Traffic campaign objective

There are 3 phases when setting up an Ad campaign on Facebook or Instagram. They are Campaigns, Adsets, and Ads.

❖ Click the green "+create" button on your Ads Manager dashboard.

❖ Select a "Traffic" objective and click on the "Continue" button at the campaign level.

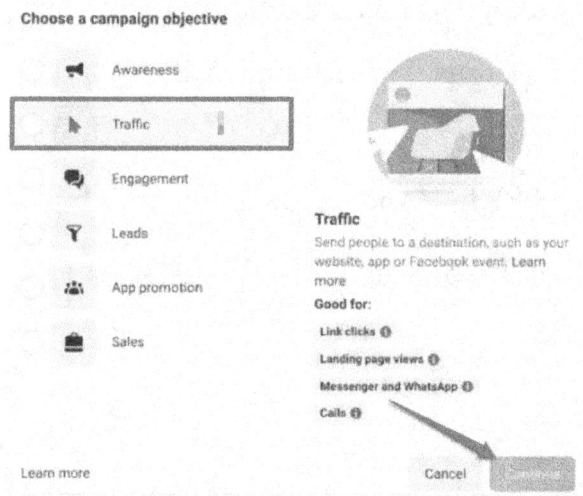

❖ Write a name for your campaign; I wrote "IG Traffic Test."

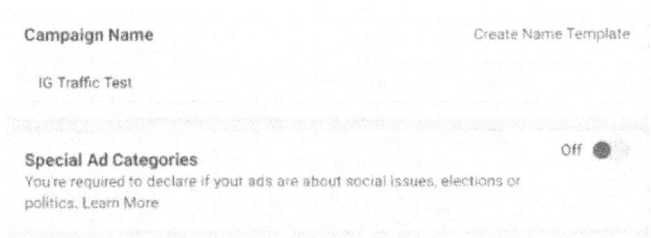

❖ Select "website" as your destination under Traffic on the Adset level.

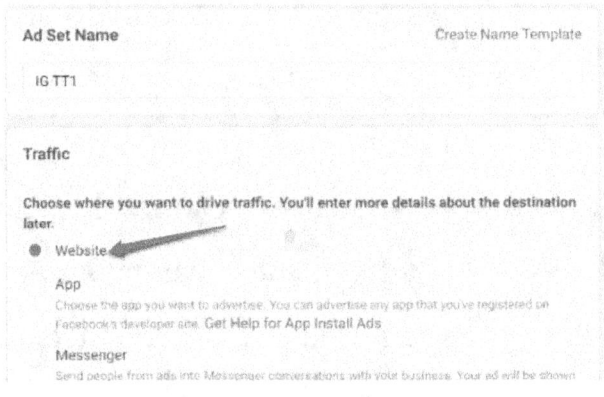

❖ Choose "Budget and Schedule."

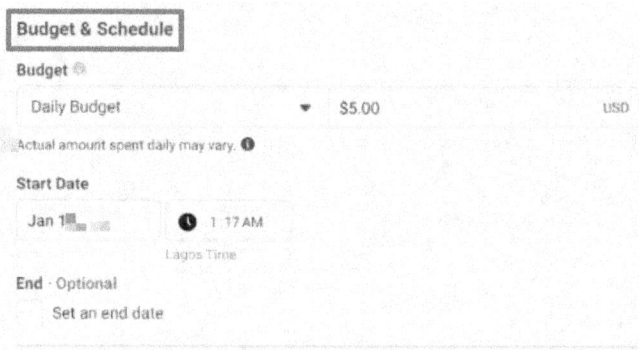

❖ Audiences, locations, age, gender, etc. are next. When aiming for a specific location, always be specific. Additionally, keep an eye on the audience definition to your right.

➢ Audiences: Before launching your advertising campaign, you are advised to conduct audience research. Click on "Audience Insights" under "Business Tools."

You will enter your location, age range, and interests to determine your exact preference for the good or service you're providing.

➢ Detailed Targeting: Based on their interests, actions, and activities, you will target specific people. As an illustration, if you enjoy baking cakes, Facebook offers you a variety of targeting options here. There is a 25-limit option.

Detailed Targeting
Include people who match ❶

Q cake	Suggestions Browse
Cake	Interests
Cake Decorator	Job Title
Cake Maker	Job Title
Cake (band)	Interests
Pancake	Interests

You may not be aware of the numerous targeting options available. I'll introduce you to the Facebook interest-targeting tool website "Enginescout" to learn more about your options.

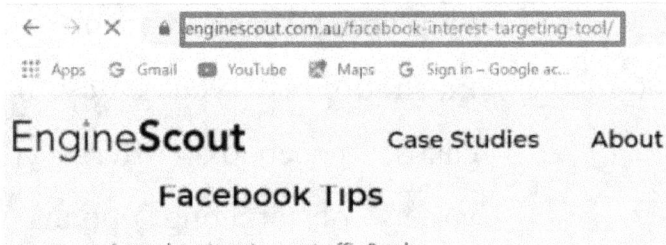

The website is a free resource for Facebook interest targeting. It will reveal which keyword category each one belongs to based on keywords, audience size, and industry. Your audience can then be saved for retargeting purposes.

❖ Use "Manual Placements" under the placement section. Leave "Automatic Placements" off.

➢ Device: Because most people use Instagram on mobile devices, select only "Mobile" and uncheck "Desktop." Additionally, limit the platform to Instagram only.

Select both if you want your advertisement to appear on both feeds and stories, or just one of them. Depending on your decision.

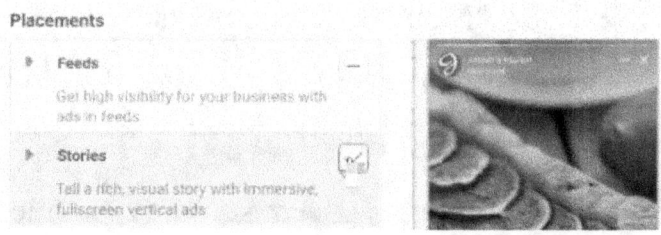

❖ Leave it on "Link Clicks" under Optimization and Delivery. Then, Click on the "Next" button.

❖ The Facebook page you are running the advertisement to must be chosen on the Ad level; if you linked your Instagram page to your Facebook page before running your ad campaign, Instagram will then be selected automatically.

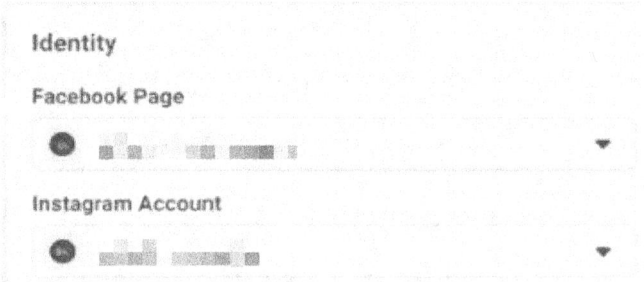

❖ I'll choose "Single Image or Video" from the options available, such as Carousel and Collection, in the ad setup section.

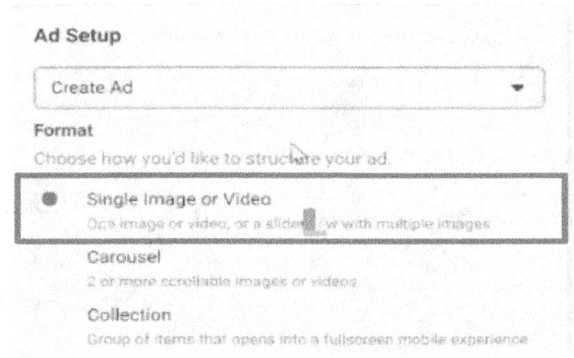

➢ Media: Click "Select videos" from the menu, and choose a video from your gallery. Toggle on the button for "Optimise creative for each person" which allows Facebook to change the video or photo very slightly depending on what specific audience habits are on both Facebook and Instagram.

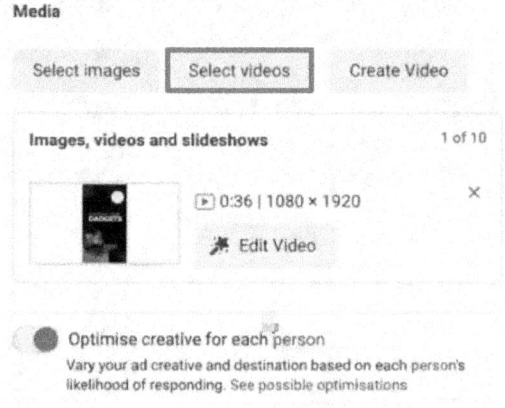

Note: *Always use square videos with a 1:1 aspect ratio. From your computer, upload your prepared video.*

➢ Primary Text: Adhere to the same steps as they were outlined in the Facebook sales ad campaign's primary text.

➢ Headlines: Follow the same procedure as was described for Facebook sales ad campaign's headlines.

➢ Destination: You will choose "website" (I used my Instagram link in this instance) and enter the URL for your website.

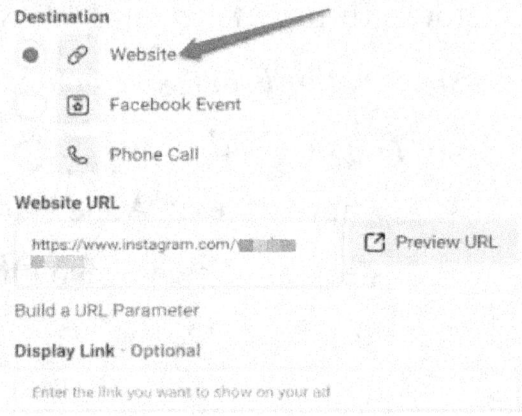

➢ Call-to-Action: Select the most effective CTA for your advertising campaign and ad copy.

❖ The "Publish" button should be clicked.

Chapter 13

Common Errors to Avoid When Running Instagram Advertisements and Best Practices for Instagram Ads Creative.

Let's look at a few common errors that advertisers make when running Instagram ads.

1. Using the **"Promote"** button directly on your Instagram account.

Question: *Why should Instagram ads not be done by clicking directly on the Promote button from a specific post?*

Answer: *This is due to its targeting capabilities and audience coverage having some restrictions. As a result, it is ineffective. However, the best method is to go through Facebook Business Manager.*

2. Using Instagram Ads to increase follower count.
3. Using only image ads.
4. Combining Feed and Story Ad: It is advised to separate them since they have different formats.
5. Not carrying out A/B testing.

Guidelines for creating effective Instagram ads

1. For any Instagram video, your Instagram advertisements should last between 10 and 15 seconds. On the same video setup, your logo, products, and CTA must all be visible.

2. Always include a caption in your Instagram advertisement videos.

3. Make sure to revise your creativity every three to four weeks.

4. Make sure your creative is consistent with your brand, for example, by matching the background color of your products.

5. The most effective type of content is user-generated

Pro tips for 15-second Instagram ads in story format

a. Within the first three seconds, grab the audience's attention with succinct and instructive text.

b. Ensure that the video ad content you create has captions, such as a description, title, or subtitle.

c. Keep text as concise and descriptive as possible

d. Make an advertisement that organically fits into your viewers' feeds.

e. Utilize user-generated content, endorsements, or influencers

f. Very crucially, add a call-to-action to your Instagram ad, such as "Shop Now," "Get Offer," "Learn More," "Swipe Up," etc.

g. Use a desktop or mobile app to filter user comments and feedback on your ads and add emoji descriptions.

Chapter 14

The Pros and Cons of Using Instagram Advertisements.

Using Instagram ads may seem like the next logical step for your business if you've been using the platform for a while and have seen business advertisements appear in your feed. Instagram can be a great platform for advertising because it allows you to run ads that can increase the number of people who see your posts and grow your brand through visually stimulating organic content. Instagram ads support website traffic and brand awareness growth.

However, there are drawbacks to Instagram advertising as well, particularly when compared to Facebook, its more established big sister platform. Additionally, linking on Instagram has been found to be less successful than on Facebook and Instagram ads are less sophisticated than those on Facebook. Due to its smaller user base than Facebook, Instagram may be a less effective advertising platform.

Before your business makes the switch to Instagram advertising, it's crucial to weigh the advantages and disadvantages of doing so.

The Pros of Using Instagram Advertising

1. Instagram Ads Increase Website Visits.

With Instagram ads, your business can include clickable links in a promoted post, unlike regular, organic Instagram posts. Consider advertising on Instagram for this important reason. When promoting a post, having the option to include a call-to-action and a link is extremely beneficial for increasing website traffic. This functionality is not available for posts that are not promoted as advertisements.

2. Instagram Advertising Increases Awareness

Breaking through the clutter of millions of posts to be seen is the biggest challenge for any business using social media marketing. The quickest and most efficient way to accomplish this is through pay-to-play. You must produce engaging Instagram posts if you want people to follow you and interact with you. It does not guarantee that you will be followed or that people will interact with you just because you paid to have your post appear in the feed of your target audience. Curating a fantastic Instagram feed to attract audiences and achieve the desired engagement requires a lot of creativity and dedication. By ensuring that people see your posts, Instagram ads can assist you in getting there.

3. Instagram Advertising Increases Brand Awareness.

When you pay to advertise on Instagram, your post will show up in the newsfeed of your intended audience without being overly intrusive or disruptive. When a user is watching the Instagram stories of users they follow, an advertisement for your product or service will automatically appear in between the stories. These discrete advertisements can significantly raise consumer awareness of your business's brand.

Your business can choose its budget, audience, and Instagram ad duration, just like it can with

Facebook advertising. You can specify demographics like age range, gender, location, and interests when you build your audience. This enables you to reach the people most likely to be interested in what you are advertising by showing your ads to a specific audience.

4. Instagram Provides Advertising Options. Businesses can create Instagram ads using their Facebook Ads Manager accounts, which is another benefit of using Instagram for advertising. Instagram ads benefit from leveraging Facebook Ads, the most sophisticated social media ad platform currently available. Instagram gives you the option to advertise based on objectives like promoting link clicks, attracting visitors to your business's Instagram profile, and raising visibility.

Additionally, there are various options for advertisements on Instagram. Businesses can advertise using videos, single images, or multi-image carousel ads. Instagram Stories advertising is an additional choice! The options for advertising on the app will grow over time because Instagram is constantly releasing new features.

The Cons of Using Instagram Advertising

1. Links From Instagram Are Less Powerful Than Links From Facebook.

Since users cannot include a clickable link in their posts, Instagram is not a platform that encourages users to click. This indicates that a billion users of Instagram never anticipate clicking, instead double tapping to express their liking for the posts they see.

A business can include a link in a post by boosting it. This is a tremendous benefit for businesses that want to increase traffic to their websites. However, research indicates that link clicks on Instagram are currently less common than on Facebook. Instagram users frequently scroll through their feeds, tap a post twice to like it, and then keep going.

Instagram is primarily visual, which is advantageous in many ways, but it also has a drawback in that it makes it simple to view and like an Instagram photo without reading the caption. Although you can include clickable links in your Instagram advertisements, they are less likely to be used than links in a Facebook advertisement. If your objective is to increase website traffic, you should compare the effectiveness of Facebook and Instagram ads.

2. Instagram's User Base is Small.

Instagram has over a billion active monthly users, making it a popular platform that makes sense to advertise on. Given that so many users are actively using the platform, why not? Perhaps, but it's important to dig a little deeper into the information. Although Instagram has a sizable user base, the majority of its users are young adults (18–29). If you are a brand looking to connect with young people, this is fantastic.

But because many of their potential customers aren't using the app, at least not actively, brands aiming at an older audience might be reluctant to spend money on Instagram advertisements. These businesses might decide that spending more time and money on Facebook advertising is more beneficial. My recommendation is to test

151

Instagram ads and compare them to comparable ads placed on Facebook or other platforms to see if you get the best results in reaching your target audience.

3. Instagram Ad Features Are Less Sophisticated.

Instagram advertising is relatively simple, so that's a benefit, right? Contrarily, less complex Instagram ads don't always have the same features as more complex Facebook ads, so this isn't always the case. There is no option on Instagram for creating a "Like" ad campaign that will increase your page's followers directly, as there is on Facebook. Additionally, Facebook ads permit more specificity than Instagram ads do.

Even though your business can use Facebook Ads Manager for Instagram advertising, there are currently fewer options available on Instagram than on Facebook. Instagram ads can still be beneficial and effective, but perhaps not to the same extent as Facebook ads. So, once more, you're left to consider whether it might be better for your business to concentrate its efforts on other ad platforms.

Given the advantages and disadvantages of Instagram ads, choosing whether or not to use them can seem difficult. Review the Instagram advertising platform, and if you think it might help you achieve your objectives, try it out. The best way to determine whether a social media advertising platform is effective for your business's objectives is through testing. Regardless of any list of benefits or drawbacks, the only surefire way to determine whether a platform is right for you is to use it.

Conclusion

With Instagram Ads, you'll be able to develop comprehensive campaigns for users at every stage of the sales process, more successfully raise brand awareness, and spark conversations all at once. You should think about using Instagram ads for the following three reasons:

❖ Since Instagram Ads and Facebook Ads are completely integrated, you can take advantage of the high engagement on Instagram as well as Facebook's superior campaign customization options, formatting options, and targeting options.

❖ Users of Instagram are eager and interested to interact with businesses and their advertisements. Yotpo estimates that

Instagram users are 120x more likely than Twitter users to interact with branded content, and 58x more likely to do so on Instagram than on Facebook.

❖ However, Yotpo found that Instagram users are 2.8 times more likely to remember Instagram ads than they are to remember ads from any other social network. This suggests that Instagram users are not just more willing to engage. They are more likely to remember the advertisement in addition to being more likely to click on or like it.

To guarantee that your content is seen, Instagram Ads is the perfect solution.

www.ingramcontent.com/pod-product-compliance
Lightning Source LLC
Chambersburg PA
CBHW071136220526

45467CB00015B/1139